The 'at' Bat

By Viola & Zaida Stefano

VeeZee Publications

Copyright © VeeZee Publications Pty. Ltd. 2025
First published in Australia in 2025
by VeeZee Publications Pty. Ltd.
veezeepublications.com

The right of Viola Stefano to be identified as the author of this work have been asserted by her in accordance with the **Copyright Amendment (Moral Rights) Act 2000.**

All rights reserved. Apart from any use as permitted by the author & under the **Copyright Act 1968**, no part may be reproduced, copied, scanned, stored in a retrieval system, recorded, or shared, by any means or in any form, without prior written & signed authorization from the publisher.

ISBN: 978-1-923120-24-2

A catalogue record of this book is available from the **National Library of Australia.**

Author: Viola Stefano
Illustrations, cover & internal designs: Zaida Stefano

Illustrations copyright © Zaida Stefano 2025
Design copyright © Zaida Stefano 2025

Disclaimer: The content presented in this book is meant for educational purposes only. The author & publisher claim no accountability to any entity or person for any liability, damage, or loss caused or assumed to be caused directly or indirectly as a consequence of the application, use, or interpretation of the material in this book.

Core words used in this book

I	want	**can**	stop	look
like	more	he	go	**see**
here	what	**do**	**the**	**and**
out	where	**we**	it	up
not	**they**	when	**that**	down
she	now	them	**is**	put
help	off	**you**	yes	**on**
turn	who	this	no	why
done	make	**a**	to	under
come	in	some	which	there
open	get	good	same	home

The fat bat sat on the mat.

The fat bat sat with a fat cat.

The fat bat can see a rat.

The fat cat can see that rat.

The fat bat and the fat cat can see the rat.

That rat is fat.

The rat can see the bat

and the cat on the mat.

I like the bat, the cat and the rat.

You like the bat, the cat and the rat.

We like the bat, the cat and the rat.

Do they like the bat, the cat and the rat?

Words that end in 'at' in this book

fat	bat	rat
cat	mat	that
	sat	

Words with 'a' in this book

and	can

We hope you had fun reading!

Learning made easy with VeeZee

VeeZee Publications

Wait, there's more!

Visit our website for information about our range of readers & supporting products.

veezeepublications.com

www.ingramcontent.com/pod-product-compliance
Lightning Source LLC
Chambersburg PA
CBHW040301100526
44584CB00004BA/301